SwanSong

Nathan Evans

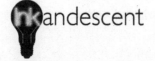

BIOGRAPHY

Nathan's shows include *I Love You But We Only Have Fourteen Minutes To Save The Earth*, *Flights of Fancy* and *7 Deadly Sins* with The Tiger Lillies (all at Soho Theatre). His new solo show *Foreign Affairs* opens at Voila! Festival in November 2018.

Productions for the Royal Vauxhall Tavern include *VauxhallVille* (2006-8), *A Pantomime Trilogy* (2007-9) and *Dave's Drop-In Centre* (2009) with David Hoyle. Other projects with David include *Theatre of Therapy* (Chelsea Theatre), *We're Not In Kansas Any More* (Southbank Centre) and *You Made Me Love You* (film series, BFI Mediatheque).

As director, he's worked on plays including *Breaking the Silence* (Arcola Theatre), *Femme Fatale* (Wilton's) and *The Novice Detective* (Contact). As performer, he's worked at venues including ICA, BAC, Little Angel, Roundhouse, Traverse, Madame Jojo's, Hoxton Hall, Komedia, Bistrotheque, Bethnal Green Working Men's Club, Pleasance, Wonderground, Artsadmin, Stratford Circus, Latitude, Glastonbury and Aldeburgh festivals. He was also part of Duckie's Olivier award-winning *C'est Barbican*.

Films include *Curtains* (Flare Film Festival), *Rock 'n' Roll Suicide* (Lo-Budget Award, London Short Film Festival) and *The Significant Death of Quentin Crisp* (Channel 4, tour with British Council).

Nathan's first poetry collection, *Threads,* is published by Inkandescent and was longlisted for the Polari First Book Prize. His second, *An Anthropozine*, is due in 2019. He's been principle oboe with London Gay Symphony Orchestra for over twenty years and studied Fine Art at Oxford University.

He lives and works in London.

www.nathanevans.co.uk

Inkandescent

Published by Inkandescent, 2018

A CIP catalogue record for this book
is available from the British Library

Printed in the UK by Clays Ltd, St Ives plc

ISBN 978-1-912620-01-2 (paperback)

MIX
Paper from
responsible sources
FSC® C018072

1 3 5 7 9 10 8 6 4 2

www.inkandescent.co.uk

for all those who started the fight
for all our rights, thank you

Lavinia Co-op (Joan) trained at London School of Contemporary Dance and was a founding member of the seminal Bloolips Theatre Company whose shows, which included *The Ugly Duckling*, *Lust in Space* and *Get Hur*, toured the UK and internationally. Living and working in New York for many years, Lavinia performed at venues like La Mama, PS 122 and TNC, with artists such as Hot Peaches and Anohni, and on many a GoGo box, also appearing in music videos (Bat For Lashes, Magic Lantern) and films by directors including Ira Sachs and Sally Potter. Lav is an acclaimed solo performer whose shows include *Installations In Stilettos* and, most recently, *Up Yours*, which premiered at the Purcell Room and will tour in 2019.

David Meyer (Jim) was a founder member of the Lindsay Kemp Company, playing Claire in Genet's *Maids* with his twin brother Tony as Solange and Lindsay as Madame at the Traverse and Bush Theatres. Their next show *Flowers*, inspired by Genet, went to the West End and Broadway. The company then toured South America, Europe. Australia and the Far East. David played Demetrius in the world tour of Peter Brook's legendary RSC production of *A Midsummer Night's Dream*. Subsequent Shakespeare roles include Hamlet for Steven Berkoff and Ferdinand, emerging naked from a very cold North Sea in Derek Jarman's *The Tempest*. He's appeared as a knife-throwing Bond villain in *Octopussy*, as a restoration fop in Peter Greenaway's *The Draughtsman's Contract*, as a Gestapo agent interviewing Mick Jagger's drag queen, Greta in the film of Martin Sherman's *Bent*, as Ben Whishaw's father in *London Spy* on BBC, and a beleaguered stage manager in the Olivier-nominated *Pagliacci* for ENO. He's directed operas by Michael Nyman and Harrison Birtwistle at the Donmar Warehouse, and Britten's *A Midsummer Night's Dream* at Sadler's Wells.

Nathanael Campbell (Craig) has theatre credits which include: *Guys & Dolls* (Royal Exchange); *Sunny Afternoon* (UK Tour); *Somewhere in England* (Eastern Angles/UK tour); *All That Lives* (Oval House); *When Blair Had Bush and Bunga* (Edinburgh Festival); *We Raise Our Hands in the Sanctuary* (Albany); *Arrivals2* (Irish Tour); *Romeo and Juliet* and *Twelfth Night* (UK tour) and *Macbeth* (UK and International Tour). Television credits include: *West Side Story* (BBC). He trained at Italia Conti Academy.

Clarisse M. Kye (producer) is also a performer, a writer and the founder of collaborative theatre company 89th Productions, whose projects have been funded by the Arts Council and developed with theatres such as Arcola, Cockpit and Pleasance. *www.89thproductions.com*

Emma Robinson (set/costume designer) studied Design for Performance at Wimbledon College of Art. She has since gone on to work for companies such as The Royal Opera House, The Royal Court, Complicite, Fevered Sleep and Historic Royal Palaces, specialising in designing for devised theatre and making work in the rehearsal room, most recently with The Plasticine Men on *Engine Break* at the New Diorama. Her work as a Stage Manager on *The Royal Court's The Kid Stays In The Picture* earned her an Outstanding Stage Management nomination.

Zak Macro (lighting designer) studied at The Royal Central School of Speech and Drama and now works as a designer and re-lighter for many companies, touring nationally and internationally. His work spans dance, music, theatre and opera. Recent credits include *Extinguished Things* (Summerhall), *Swing Sister Swing* (Arcola Theatre), *NOISE* (The Old Rep), White Guy On The Bus (*The Finborough*), *Jenufa* (The ENO at Lilian Baylis), *Death Of A Hunter* (Finborough) and *Until The Lions* (Akram Khan Company World Tour) *www.zak-macro.com*

Justin David (publicity designer/photographer) lives and works in East London. He studied BA Graphic Communication at the University of Northampton and later MA Creative and Life Writing at Goldsmiths. He is the co-founder of Inkandescent. His photos have been widely published in magazines and on the covers of books. His photography/ poetry collaboration with Nathan Evans, *Threads*, was longlisted for the Polari First Book Prize. *www.justindavid.co.uk*

Anna Goodman (publicist) launched Abstrakt Publicity in 1999 and continues to enjoy working with a diverse cross-section of artists and projects. Current clients include *Breakin' Convention*: Sadler's Wells international hip hop dance festival, Scottee, Marisa Carnesky, Andrew Logan's *Alternative Miss World* at Shakespeare's Globe, Compass Festival Leeds, Stopgap Dance Company and Brighton's Marlborough Theatre. *www.abstraktpublicity.co.uk*

INTRODUCTION

I first outlined *SwanSong* in 2010, in response to horror stories I'd heard about LGBT+ elders entering care. The majority of LGBT+ people don't have children to look after them as they're ageing and are therefore especially dependent on the care system. There will likely be at least one LGBT+ person in every care home in the country, but many choose to hide their sexuality for fear of how they'll be treated by straight peers—whose prejudices may not have shifted with the times—and staff whose faith or cultures may not be entirely approving.

I wanted to write a story about someone who simply refuses to go back in the closet and is suddenly thrown into conflict with some of the people they've probably spent the last half-century avoiding. I wanted to write about them inspiring someone else to come back out again. I wanted to write about two gentlemen falling in love in a care home. I thought it was about bloody time.

We've seen plenty of stories about young gay love and, recently, stories of mature straight love to reflect our aging demographics but mature gay people are often overlooked by the media—gay media especially—and one might be forgiven for thinking we queers melt like wicked witches at age fifty. In the absence of some form of cross-generational awareness, it's easy for our younger brothers and sisters to be complacent about our current acceptance, forgetting that without those pioneers who began the fight for equal rights five decades back this acceptance could not exist. I wanted to address this.

I spent some time researching—visiting care homes and the

Opening Doors London social group for LGBT+ over-fifties—after that outline. The script's first incarnation was as a feature film called *The Grey Liberation Front* which was read at Soho Theatre in 2012 by actors including Bette Bourne, Richard Wilson, Nina Wadia and Chris New – actors secured through the enthusiasm of my casting director friend Gary Davy. Sadly, his ardour wasn't shared universally by the industry – a few years and many funding applications later, just a fraction of the budget had been raised.

In that first manifestation, Joan—my protagonist—insists we must *never accept defeat*. I took that to heart and redrafted the story first as a radio play, then a stage play. It didn't fare any better as either until the King's Head Theatre programmed *SwanSong*—as it was retitled—for their *Queer Festival 2017*, where it was given a staged reading by Lavinia Co-op, John Atterbury and Alexis Gregory. The audience response was amazing (and something of a vindication). The play simply had to have a full production.

Which brings us—via a redraft, a recast, and a greatly appreciated Arts Council grant—to 2018 and the play's much anticipated (by me at least) presentation and publication.

Never accept defeat.

Nathan Evans, August 2018

Cast

Joan   Lavinia Co-op
Jim   David Meyer
Craig   Nathanael Campbell

Premiered at the Royal Vauxhall Tavern on Wednesday 17 October 2018 as part of *And What? Queer. Arts. Festival*, then toured to the Marlborough Theatre, Brighton.

Characters

Joan, male, white, seventies
Jim, male, white, seventies
Craig, male, black, twenties

Setting

a care home

Scene 1

Mozart's 'You Who Know What Love Is' fades down as lights come up to reveal, to one side, Joan's room, to the other, Jim's.

In Jim's room, a suitcase stands by the door. **Jim**, *in dressing gown and slippers, is studying an ancient book on the internet.*

In Joan's room, clothes are colourfully overflowing from an open case. **Joan**'s *apparel is a mixture of male and female. He's studying a picture.*

Joan Well, look at you.

Joan *stands the picture beside his record player.*

Joan Look. At. You.

Joan *looks around and sighs.*

Joan If only you knew.

A knock. **Joan** *hesitates.*

Joan Who is it?

Craig Room service!

Craig *comes in. There's a tray in his hand with two plastic cups on it, one containing water and the other pills.*

Joan I don't remember ordering you in.

Craig No-one round here remembers anything.

Joan Ha!

Craig Craig. I'm the deputy manager.

Craig *offers his hand.* **Joan** *takes it, kisses it.*

Joan The pleasure is all mine.

Craig And you must be John?

Joan Joan, please.

Craig *nods, removes his hand.*

Craig So—Joan—I can see you're settling in?

Joan It's like home from home!

Joan *plucks some records from the case.*

Craig Yeah, don't go blasting those this time of night. Old dears need their beauty sleep. You meet any of our other residents yet?

Joan I have that to look forward to.

Craig Lucky you. Cocktail. (*rattles pill cup*) Madam or sir, which do you prefer?

Joan I prefer to savour the individual flavours. (*picking out a* *pill*) What's this one?

Craig Enalapril.

Joan (*like a dirty word*) Enalapril. And what does that do?

Craig For your heart, I think.

Joan (*picking out another*) And this one?

Craig Reminyl.

Joan (*savouring every syllable*) Re-mi-nyl.

Craig That's for your head. And that one's…

Joan *reaches for the final pill.*

Craig …just aspirin. Bottoms up!

Joan *takes the water cup* **Craig** *offers, swallows the pills.* **Craig** *spots the picture.*

Craig Who's this?

Joan (*sucking in his stomach*) Guess.

Craig No!

Joan I was quite a dish.

Craig When was it taken?

Joan That, my dear, was the very first gay pride demonstration. 1972.

Craig Not sure about that hair though.

Joan Like 'em butch, do you?

Craig Yeah. I like big butch daddy bears.

Joan (*letting stomach out again*) So am I in with a chance then?

Craig (*laughing*) I'm a married man.

Joan *frowns.* **Craig** *gathers the cups.*

Craig My husband is horribly jealous of me working around all you hot older men.

Joan And how old are you, if you don't mind me asking?

Craig How old do you think I am?

Joan Sixteen or seventeen?

Craig I'm twenty-nine.

Joan Isn't that a little young to be settling down?

Craig I've found the man I want to spend the rest of my life with.

Joan How very hetero-normative.

Craig Sorry?

Joan Sounds lovely.

Craig *takes Joan's cups back.*

Jim Search engine...

Jim *looks up from his book.*

Craig Call me if you need anything.

Craig *indicates the alarm.*

Jim That's what I thought it was when I heard the siren.

Joan It's like the Garden of Eden.

Craig Sweet dreams.

Craig *leaves.* **Joan** *looks after him.*

Joan Once upon a time...

Jim *looks to his bookmark.*

Jim I'd forgotten she cleans on a Wednesday morning.
Must have called the ambulance men.

Jim *looks to his wrist.*

Joan   (to photo) My dear, once upon a time she would have been paying.

Joan laughs and selects a record.

A knock. **Jim** *conceals the mark within his book.*

Jim   Come in!

Jim *places the book down.* **Craig** *comes in.*

Craig   Sorry I'm late. Been chatting to your new neighbour.

Jim   I thought I could hear someone next door. The walls are so thin here.

Craig   He's unpacking. (*nodding to case*) How long has it been?

Craig *offers the tray in his hand.* **Jim** *takes the pills.* **Craig** *waits for him to swallow them.*

Craig   Still reading about the Internet?

Craig *picks the book up, flicks through it.*

Jim   One has to keep up with the latest developments if one's to find a position.

Craig   You know, I could always show you how to get online. (*finding bookmark*) Who's this?

Jim (*beat*) None of your business.

Craig Right.

Craig *puts the book down, takes the cups back and heads to the door.*

Craig Night!

Craig *leaves.* **Jim** *looks after him.*

Joan *has put on 'Spring' from Strauss' 'Four Last Songs', hums along.*

Jim *turns, listens.*

Joan *finds his handbag, finds a joint inside it and steps onto his balcony, moonlit.*

Hearing this, **Jim** *reaches for his stick, gets up.*

Joan *is smoking when he hears* **Jim** *step onto his own balcony.*

Joan Aren't they glorious? The roses.

Jim *just stares at him.*

Joan Joan. I would offer you my hand, but alas the distance between us is too vast. It reminds me of the Genet film. What was it called again? There's these guys in cells and they toss flowers to each other through the bars in the windows. So beautiful. And then they blow smoke through a hole in the wall.

Jim Smoking is not permitted, except…

Joan I know darling, but it helps me sleep.

Jim Well your music is preventing me from sleeping. Kindly turn it down or I shall raise the alarm. Thank you, and good evening.

He goes in, leaving **Joan** *chuckling.* **Joan** *takes another toke as the music swells and lights fade.*

Scene 2

Next evening. **Joan** *is looking for something.*

Jim *looks up from his book.*

Jim I'll get on top of it soon. I promise. I just…

Jim *looks down, adjusts his dressing gown.*

Jim I can't quite concentrate tonight.

A knock. **Jim** *covers his lap with the book.*

Jim Come in!

Craig *comes in, tray in hand.*

Craig So a little bird tells me that Jimmy has been a bad boy. Not left his room all day.

Jim *avoids eye contact, takes the cups.*

Craig Are you okay?

Jim I didn't feel like socialising.

Craig Shame. Chairobics this morning and dinner was jerk chicken.

Jim *grimaces.*

Craig Perhaps we need to up your dosage again.

Jim *glances at him.*

Craig We'll have to get the doctor in.

Jim *gulps the pills down.*

Craig You don't want us to get the doctor in?

Jim *shakes his head.*

Craig We'll see you for breakfast then.

Beat. **Jim** *nods.* **Craig** *takes the cups back.*

Craig Good man. You know, you should try talking to Eileen.

Jim Eileen?

Craig Mm. I think she's got a soft spot.

Jim (*beat*) Right.

Craig Oh, come on. She's not bad looking. Decent pair. Still got her own hair.

Jim I… don't think it would be right to start a relationship.

Craig And why is that?

Jim I don't think I'll be here long enough to sustain it.

Craig (*shaking his head*) Night!

He exits. **Jim** *looks after him.*

Joan There you are.

Joan *finds a bonnet with yellow ribbons.*

Joan A little…

Joan *wets a finger, wipes it.*

Joan Smutty, ha!

Joan *puts the hat on.*

Joan A smutty little number.

Jim *puts the light out.*

Joan *strikes a pose.*

Joan Well, get her!

A knock. **Joan** *looks to the door.*

Joan Still, shan't find much use for you in here. (*removing hat*) Who is it?

The door opens and **Craig** *comes in.*

Craig Room service.

Joan I do hope you haven't douched too thoroughly.

Craig (*beat*) You filthy…

Joan Could you give me a hand here?

Joan*'s removing the ribbons from the bonnet.*

Craig BDSM costs extra.

Joan Ha! They're for…

Craig *puts down his tray and helps* **Joan** *with the ribbons.*

Joan What is her name – white hair, highly flammable housecoat thing?

Craig Winifred?

Joan That's the one. She's knitting some booties for… Well, she didn't seem certain if it was a granddaughter or son. So she's gone for lemon. I suggested ribbons, but she seemed concerned about what might happen if it was a boy then. I told her, some boys like ribbons.

Joan *waves the released ribbons.*

Craig So you made a friend?

Joan Darling, all my friends are in the ground.

Craig (*offering tray*) Here.

Joan No, poor dear. I think she was just grateful someone had spoken to her.

Joan *knocks the pills back. A rising triplet emerges from Craig's pocket.* **Craig** *blushes.*

Craig Thought I'd turned that off.

Craig *turns his phone off and slips it back in his pocket.* **Joan** *smirks, swigs water.*

Craig So you meet anyone else?

Joan Let's just say that operation shock and awe has commenced.

Joan *returns the cups to the tray.*

Craig Right. (*leaving*) Night!

Craig *leaves.* **Joan** *goes to put a record on.*

Joan Well. (*to photo*) Perhaps little miss take-him-home-to-meet-your-mum-and-two-point-four-fluffy-kittens isn't quite so straight-acting as she seems.

Bizet's 'Love is a Rebellious Bird' begins, **Joan** *lipynchs along.*

Jim *turns his light on.*

Joan *grabs a scarf, does a toreador dance.*

Jim *reaches for his stick, bangs with it.*

Joan *looks at the wall, smiles and nudges up the volume. Waits for another bang.*

Jim *hesitates, discards his stick.*

Joan *discards his scarf in disappointment. Reaches for his handbag.*

Jim *reaches for the alarm. Lights and music snap out as he sounds it.*

Scene 3

Next evening. **Joan** *is sat, hand on heart, a half-rolled joint on his lap.*

Jim *is scrutinising a newspaper.*

Joan We fought them in the playground. We fought them in the police station. And we shall fight them in the old people's home…

A knock.

Joan Come in!

The door opens and **Craig** *comes in.*

Craig So, a little bird tells me Joanie's been a bad girl—again—fighting in the playground.

Joan *has returned to rolling his joint.*

Craig What are you doing?

Joan You any good at rolling?

Craig Is that…?

Joan Medicinal, yes.

Craig Joan, I can't let you…

Joan Fuck off.

Craig Joan, I'm just doing my job.

Joan Then go get on with it!

Craig *sighs in exasperation as* **Joan** *continues rolling.*

Joan Darling, don't stand there gawping.

Craig Joan…

Joan There must be plenty of gentlemen to gawp at on your phone.

Craig (*beat*) Joan, seriously…

Joan So tell me, are you open or is it old-fashioned adultery?

Craig I…

Joan And does the Taliban know you've been Grinding on duty?

Craig The Taliban?

Joan Big boss. Her in the headscarf.

Craig Rachida.

Joan I'm sure she'd be tickled pink by your extracurricular activities.

Joan *seals the joint.* **Craig** *looks away.*

Craig Just don't smoke in bed, alright. Don't want this place burning down in the night.

Joan *tucks the joint behind his ear.*

Joan Don't worry. Your secret's safe with me.

Craig So… What happened?

Craig *sits, offering pills.* **Joan** *takes them.*

Joan Oh, you know, just a bit of old-fashioned homophobic bullying.

Craig You don't think…?

Joan What?

Craig *(beat)* Well, what with last night's discotheque…

Joan *snorts.*

Craig Big Boss thinks you may have been winding Jim up?

Joan She would. *(returning cups)* You know yesterday I was in the garden, innocently admiring the roses and she had the nerve to say… *(imitating)* 'Are you always this flamboyant?'

Craig *laughs.*

Craig 'Is that a problem?' I said. (*imitating*) 'It's just that some of our residents may not be entirely comfortable with it.' Yeah right.

Craig So, you weren't then?

Joan I was just being who I am. That's provocation enough sometimes.

Craig (*patting Joan's knee*) Give it time, Joan. They'll come around.

Joan Darling, I've spent a lifetime waiting for the world to catch up. But time is a luxury I no longer have.

Craig Well, you seem to have brought Winifred round. (*standing*) Nice ribbons.

Joan You like?

Craig Night!

He leaves.

Jim Relevant engineering degree, or equivalent professional qualification.

Joan (*to photo*) We shall never surrender, shall we?

Jim Proven ability to interpret legislation and implement policy.

Joan Whatever the cost may be.

Jim Proven line management and excellent… IT skills. Hmm.

A knock. **Jim** *folds the paper.*

Jim Come in!

Craig Doctor's here!

Jim *looks up as* **Craig** *comes in.*

Craig Only joking. Given up on the internet then?

Jim ⋅ I wanted to see the jobs section.

Jim *takes the pills* **Craig** *offers him.*

Craig So… What happened?

Craig *sits.* **Jim** *eyes him suspiciously.*

Craig This afternoon…

Jim Oh, you mean with… Joan, is that what we're meant to call him?

Craig He says you were bullying him.

Jim I merely suggested he go sit with the women.

Craig But he's a man.

Jim Then perhaps he should start behaving like one.

Jim *hands his empty cup back.*

Craig Jim… I know it might not be what you're used to… but I have to tell you, we can't tolerate prejudice—of any kind—in this home.

Jim This is not my home.

Craig Just try to get on with him. (*standing*) Did you speak to Eileen?

Jim Is he alright? Seemed to have a problem with…

Craig His heart? He's alright. Least his heart is.

Craig *taps his head and winks.*

Craig Night!

Craig *leaves.* **Jim** *looks after him.*

Joan *puts on Mozart's 'The Vengeance of Hell Boils in My Heart', goes to the balcony, smokes.*

Jim *gets up, hesitates, goes out to the balcony.*

Joan Oh look, it's neighbourhood watch.

Jim I must ask you to please extinguish that.

Joan Fuck off!

Jim Right!

Jim *turns to go in.*

Joan Watcha gonna do, big man? Pull the alarm again?

Jim *hesitates.* **Joan** *takes a toke, blows it at him.*

Joan Well, go on then.

Jim Who the hell do you think you are? Flouncing in here with all your…

Joan I've been bullied by the best, darling. And I simply refuse to be bullied by a dribbling old man.

Jim Get out! Get out! Get out!

Joan There ain't anything gonna put this queen back in the closet again. I think you know what I'm saying.

Jim *says nothing.*

Joan You're not one of them.

Jim I don't know what you mean.

Joan I've seen where your eyes go when you don't think anyone is watching. (*he takes another toke in triumph, chants as he breaths out*) 2-4-6-8. Gay is just as good as straight.

Jim *stares.* **Joan** *smiles.*

Joan 2-4-6-8!

Jim Stop.

Joan Gay is just as good as straight!

Jim They'll hear us.

Joan 2-4-6-8!

Jim Please. I don't want…

Joan Gay is just as good as straight!

Jim Shut up! Always the same, you lot. Shouting from the rooftops and spoiling it for the others.

Joan Fuck off! You and all the other apologists. You're worse than the fucking straights.

Joan *discards his joint, goes in.* **Jim** *stares after him as the music swells and lights fade.*

Scene 4

Next evening. **Jim** *is looking out from his balcony, lost in thought.* **Joan** *steps onto his balcony.* **Jim** *looks at him.* **Joan** *looks away, goes to light his joint.*

Jim Did you ever visit the one in Regent's Park, we... He always loved roses.

Joan *looks over, lowers his lighter.*

Joan Queen Mary's Rose Garden?

Jim That's the one. There's another in Hyde Park.

Joan I used to cruise there at night.

Jim *blushes, looks away.*

Jim I... I'm Jim.

Jim *extends his hand.* **Joan** *smiles, extends his hand. They are far from reaching.*

Joan If I only had some flowers to swing.

Joan *mimes throwing.* **Jim**'s *reaction is slow.*

Joan Missed them.

Joan *tucks the joint behind his ear.*

Joan So… What brings you here, Jim?

Jim Oh, I shan't be here long. Just until I find a position.

Joan A position?

Jim Then I'll be going home.

Joan (*beat*) I see.

Jim Please don't tell anyone.

Joan That you're leaving?

Jim That I'm…

Joan A dirty little queer? (*laughing*) Your secret's safe with me, dear.

There's a knock at Jim's door, which they don't hear.

Jim And you? What brings you here?

Joan Danger unto myself. Or so they tell me. And, sadly, I neglected to deposit any progeny by way of insurance policy.

Jim You don't have any family?

Joan It's been some decades since they wanted anything to do with me.

Jim I'm sorry.

Joan Don't be.

Joan *waves it away.*

Jim Your rings, you have so many of them.

Joan You like 'em? You paid for 'em!

Jim *doesn't understand.*

Joan Liberace? Another closet case. You don't have any yourself?

Jim *shakes his head.*

Joan Not even the one?

Jim *(beat)* He died before we had the opportunity.

Joan I'm sorry.

Jim Did you have a partner?

Joan No-one in particular.

Another knock.

Joan Was that the door?

Jim *turns as* **Craig** *comes in.*

Craig Jim?

Jim *hurries in.*

Joan Night then.

Joan *reaches for the joint, thinks better of it.*

Jim Just admiring the garden. I do so miss my own. Must be getting overgrown. Never mind, back there soon. Are those for me, then?

Jim *takes the pills and water from the tray in* **Craig**'s *hand.*

Joan *goes in.*

Craig Sorry I'm late. There's been an incident.

Jim Right.

Craig Winifred.

Jim *replaces the cups on the tray.*

Jim Okay.

Craig Sorry.

Jim Don't suppose there was anything you could have done about it.

Craig *pats him on the shoulder.* **Jim** *flinches.*

Craig Night night.

Craig *leaves,* **Jim** *looks after him.*

Joan *puts on 'When Falling Asleep', from Strauss' 'Four Last Songs'.*

Joan Do you remember? (*to photo*) Queued for hours. Pete wanted to give up but… Standbys at the last minute. (*savouring the music*) Pure magic. (*sitting*) Poor Peter. That was before AIDA got her.

A knock.

Joan Who is it?

Craig *comes in.*

Craig Sorry I'm late, there's been an incident.

Joan Nothing fatal, I hope?

Craig Joan…

Joan *looks up, sees* **Craig** *is serious.*

Joan Oh. Anyone we know?

Craig Winifred.

Joan (*beat*) But we just saw her. It can only have been an hour…

Craig It's a long time in here.

Craig *offers the tray in his hand.*

Joan Are you sure?

Craig I have it on authority from the doctor.

Joan Surely someone should have noticed that something was wrong?

Craig Can't be everywhere at the same time.

Joan I should have noticed. I could have done something…

Craig I don't think…

Joan Did she die alone?

Craig I…

Joan (*covering eyes*) Oh, that's terrible.

Craig (*squeezing Joan's arm*) I'm sorry, Joan.

Joan Now she'll never know if it's a boy or a girl.

Craig No. (*spotting the joint and removing his hand*) Right then.

Joan Honestly that one, she'll weep at the drop of a hat pin.

Craig (*offering a pill cup*) Nightcap.

Joan Courvoisier?

Craig You'll be lucky.

Joan (*taking cup*) Well, cheers anyway.

Craig Yeah, cheers.

Craig *takes the joint.* **Joan** *splutters.*

Joan But…

Craig Not tonight. The Taliban's on to it.

Craig *puts the joint in his pocket.*

Joan How so?

Craig If you will leave the evidence beneath your window…

Joan I did?

Craig She recognised your particular shade of lipstick.

Joan But how shall I sleep?

Craig I'm sure you'll find something.

Craig *makes a wanking gesture.*

Joan   Darling, I'm too old for such things.

Craig   You know Joan, the trick to tearing up the rulebook is to not get caught doing it.

Craig *leaves.* **Joan** *looks after him.*

Jim   Poor dear.

Jim *is now sat on the bed, book open, photograph in hand.*

Jim   Look out for her.

Joan *sighs, looks to his picture.*

Joan   I do hope they like the ribbons, whatever they are.

And the violin solos as the lights fade.

Scene 5

Next evening. **Jim** *is smartly dressed, coat over arm.*

Jim You weren't joking about the record collection.

Joan Why else do you think I invited you in? Sit down.

Joan *scoops records up.* **Jim** *sits, spots the photograph.*

Jim Is that…?

Joan It is, yes.

Jim *is impressed.*

Joan Something atmospheric. Wagner perhaps?

Jim I know nothing about opera.

Joan You know I worked there?

Jim As a singer?

Joan As a costume maker.

Jim Is that where you got all yours?

Joan (*beat*) Darling, those aren't costumes. If they were, I'd be playing a part. Which I'm not. (*selecting a record and putting it on*) So what did you wear then? As a civil servant? Or were you a naked one?

41

Jim   (*beat*) I was a clothed one. In sensible shoes and a sensible suit with a sensible haircut and a sensible life… And really you must find me terribly tiresome and it's time for me to go…

Joan   Where? Home? (*laughing*) Do you really believe that?

Joan *puts Dvorak's 'Song to the Moon' on.*

Joan   (*sighing*) Dvorak. (*beat*) It's a song about the moon. How he travels around the world and looks into homes. (*pulling a joint from his handbag*) Shall we see if he's looking into this one?

Jim   (*beat*) Smoking isn't permitted, except in…

Joan   Rules are there to be broken.

Joan *goes to the balcony.* **Jim** *looks after him, hesitates, follows* **Joan**, *who offers the joint.*

Joan   A little chink in the wall between us?

Jim   I…

Joan   Learn to live before you die.

Jim *tentatively takes the joint and puts it to his lips, sucks, coughs.* **Joan** *laughs. They don't hear the knock.*

Joan   I'll give you a blowback.

Jim A what?

Joan Just put it in your mouth. Said the actor to the bishop.

Jim *hesitates, does as told.*

Joan Now breathe in as I breathe out.

Joan *moves in.* **Jim** *pulls back.* **Joan** *stops him.*

Joan On the count of three.

Joan *puts his mouth around the lit end of the joint. Their eyes meet, their lips almost.* **Joan** *speaks without moving his.*

Joan One, two, three…

Joan *breathes out,* **Jim** *breathes in. Time is suspended a moment.*

Craig (*off*) Room service!

Craig *enters, sees them.* **Jim** *explodes coughing, pulls back.* **Joan** *takes the joint from his mouth, laughs, sees* **Craig** *watching. Rubs* **Jim**'s *back.*

Joan (*sotto voce*) You should go. There's going to be trouble.

Jim What sort of trouble?

Jim *turns to see* **Craig**.

Joan You'll have to make your own introductions. You know I'm simply terrible with names.

Craig I'm disappointed in you, Jim.

Jim I... I was just leaving.

Craig *nods, passes him his coat and cane.*

Craig Should steer clear of this one. Bad influence.

Jim Please don't tell anyone.

Joan *continues smoking.*

Jim If I get a conviction, I'll never work again.

Joan *laughs.*

Jim Perhaps it doesn't matter for a career in the theatre. But if one's a senior engineer...

Craig *guides him out.*

Jim Oh, now I'll never get out of here.

Craig I'll be in to see you just as soon as I've finished with Joan.

Craig *turns to* **Joan**, *who takes a last toke.* **Craig** *offers him a pill cup.*

Craig Swap – your drugs for mine.

Joan *shakes his head.*

Craig Those are the rules and you'll have to learn to live by them.

Joan *discards the joint in the garden.*

Craig I lied for you, Joan. Told her I couldn't find anything, that I was certain you weren't smoking in your room, that probably some kids had broken in the garden… You promised to be discreet about it. And then I find you pushing it on one of our most vulnerable residents.

Jim *enters his own room, turns the light on.*

Craig I mean, poor Jim… probably doesn't know what's hit him. (*rattling the cup*) Joan, please, my job is on the line.

Joan You know, in my day the queers wanted to be different. You lot just want to fit in. We didn't want to get by in the world as it existed. We wanted to recreate it in our own image.

Craig You obviously succeeded. How else would you have ended up in this place? (*dropping pill cup*) If you want your tablets, I suggest you get down and lick them off the carpet. Knowing you, you'll probably enjoy it.

Craig *slams out. The orchestra slam in with Stravinsky's setting of 'Do Not Go Gentle into that Good Night' as* **Joan** *holds his heart and* *crumples to the carpet.*

Jim *reaches for his book, opens it at the mark.* **Craig** *looks in.* **Jim** *doesn't look up.* **Craig** *puts the cups beside him, notices the bookmark in Jim's hand.* **Jim** *looks up at him.* **Craig** *smiles, goes to pat his back then doesn't, heads out.* **Jim** *looks after him.*

Joan *picks a pill from the carpet, lifts it to smudged lips, tries to swallow it.*

Jim *looks back to the bookmark as we hit a pause in the music.*

Jim   Old fool. No one could replace you.

Joan   Never surrender.

Jim *lifts the photograph, kisses it.* **Joan** *looks to his own photo.*

Jim   We're going home now.

Joan   Never accept defeat.

As music resumes, lights fade.

Scene 6

The following afternoon. **Joan**, *head bandaged, screaming.*

Jim, *coat on, suitcase in one hand, bandage on the other, turns towards the sound.*

Joan Fascist bitch! Who the fuck does she think she…
Ah. (*putting a hand to his heart*) We've got to get out of here.
(*to photo*) We have got to get out of here. (*sits*) If only I could just tap my fucking heels together…

Jim *sets the case down. A knock. He hesitates.*

Jim Come in.

Craig *comes in.*

Craig What have you done to your hand, young man?

Jim *looks at his hand.*

Craig Do you really hate us that much?

Jim *looks back up.*

Craig Come on. Let's get that coat off.

Craig *goes to help.* **Jim** *resists. Tries to take the coat off himself.*

Craig You know, Jim, doors are locked for a reason.

Jim I was just…

Craig Trying to smash it open?

Jim *is struggling.* **Craig** *intervenes.*

Craig Sit down.

Jim *sits.* **Craig** *hangs the coat, sits.*

Craig So, what seems to be the problem?

Jim *picks at the bandage on his hand.*

Craig It's not the first time this has happened…

Joan *pulls his stash from his handbag.*

Craig Jim?

Joan *holds the stash up.*

Craig How can we help if you won't tell us what the problem is?

Joan *empties it onto the carpet from height.*

Craig You know, we can't just brush this under the carpet. Remember why you came to us in the first place…

Joan Fuck you!

Craig *and* **Jim** *look over on hearing this.*

Joan Fucking fuckers!

Joan *grinds the stash into the carpet.*

Craig Is it something to do with what happened last night?

Jim *doesn't need to say anything.*

Craig Well, don't worry, he won't be here much longer anyway.

Jim Why?

Craig Because he's disturbing the other residents.

Joan There!

Joan *sits down again.*

Craig Perhaps we should also refer you elsewhere?

For the first time, **Jim** *looks at him.*

Craig Well, you're obviously not happy here…

Jim Where?

Craig (*shrugging*) Another home.

Jim My home?

Craig You're not ever going back there again. It's about time you accepted that, Jim.

Jim *shakes his head.*

Craig Sold! Gone! Profits paying for your long-term care solution!

Jim *hangs his head.*

Craig I'm sorry, Jim.

Craig *lays a hand on* **Jim**'s *shoulder. For the first time,* **Jim** *allows it to be there.*

Craig Of course, I understand we're one of the better establishments in the area and we'll be sorry to see you leave here, but it's your decision. (*standing*) If you do decide you're staying, I do want that case unpacking.

Craig *leaves.* **Jim** *looks after him.*

A knock. **Joan** *buries his head.*

Jim *looks to the case.*

Another knock and **Craig** *comes in, stands waiting for* **Joan** *to acknowledge him.*

Jim *goes to the case.*

Craig Joan...?

Joan If you want your drugs I suggest you get down and lick them off the carpet.

Craig *sees Joan's scattered gear.*

Joan Knowing you, you'll probably enjoy it.

Jim *clicks the case open.*

Craig *furiously gathers grass in his palm.*

Craig (*under breath*) Fucking...

Joan *surreptitiously watches him, smiling.*

Jim *lifts the photo from the case.*

Jim What do you think, darling? Could this be our home?

Jim *looks around. He looks at the photo. He props it up and steps back.*

Craig *gathers the last of the grass, looks up at* **Joan**, *hesitates.*

Craig Last night... I'm sorry, my behaviour was inappropriate.

Joan (*beat*) The Taliban tell you to say that?

Craig She told me you made a complaint.

Joan Well, I'm sorry – when one is paying however many hundreds a day for hospitality, I believe one has a right to expect better service.

Craig I believe it's being paid for by her majesty's government...?

Joan And you expect me to be grateful for that? I've paid my taxes same as the straights have.

Jim *looks around, leaves his room.*

Joan What exactly is your policy on LGBT residents?

Craig It's, er... not something we've ever had to deal with before.

Joan Are you sure?

Craig (*beat*) Who are we talking about here?

Joan (*beat*) From the moment I walked through that door there's been nothing but side glances and snickers and don't you dare sit there. From you... I thought for better.

Craig *looks away.*

Craig Perhaps you might try to be more tolerant of the other residents?

Joan I will not tolerate intolerance!

Craig Well, we will not tolerate the consumption of an illegal substance. And - whilst you remain with us - you will please refrain from smoking anywhere but in the designated area. Should you find that problematic, we recommend the Smokefree service, freely available on the NHS.

Joan Whose side are you on?

Craig Oh, come on. It's the twenty-first century, Joan. The battle is won.

Craig *exits.*

Joan And who was it that fought on the frontline? (*to photo*) Who braved the opprobrium of family and friends? Got attacked in the street, arrested? And turned out to every protest whether it rained or it did not? (*to Craig, off*) Well, it wasn't you, was it?

Another knock.

Joan Now what?

Jim (*beat, off*) It's Jim.

Joan (*to himself*) And what do you want?

Jim (*beat*) Can I come in?

Joan (*sighs*) It's open!

Joan *wipes mascara, turns to see* **Jim** *with a rose in his hand.*

Jim (*beat*) Catch.

Jim *tosses the flower.* **Joan** *manages not to drop it, looks at the rose, looks at* **Jim**.

Joan It's meant to be a bunch of them.

Jim I stole it from the garden.

Joan (*tuts*) What happened to your hand?

Jim What happened to your head?

Joan I would appear we've both been in the wars.

Jim Must look a right pair.

Joan I shall wear it in my hair.

Joan *puts the rose in his hair.*

Jim I tried to break free.

Joan Really?

Jim Didn't work, obviously.

Joan You cannot mean, sir, that we are trapped here together? Ta-dah!

Jim (*beat*) You look lovely.

Joan Please! Spare me. Let's have some music, shall we…

Joan *sifts records.*

Jim Is that why you do it?

Joan Do what?

Jim The lipstick? The flamboyant clothing? Constantly putting yourself in the firing line?

Joan Here we go…

Joan *puts a record on.*

Jim Maybe I'm not the one who's self-hating.

Joan *enjoys the opening cadences of Mahler's 'Oh Little Red Rose'.*

Jim I won't let them touch you again.

Jim *takes Joan's hand in his.* **Joan** *looks at it.*

Joan Your wrist…?

Jim That's why I'm in this place.

Joan You…

Jim With Alex dead, I had no reason to live.

Jim *raises* **Joan***'s hand to his lips and kisses it.* **Joan** *laughs.*

Jim What?

Joan (*removing his hand*) I'm really not your type.

Jim What do you mean?

Joan I, my dear, am an effeminate queer. Whereas you… are a respectable homosexual.

Jim And?

Joan (*taking his arm*) Couldn't we just be friends?

Music swells and lights fade.

Scene 7

Later that evening. The sound of knocking, of snoring, of knocking again. Light spills in to reveal **Joan** *and* **Jim** *fully clothed, spooning.* **Craig** *is grossed, touched. He exits. The light wakes* **Joan**. **Craig** *returns with two pill cups, tiptoes in, freezes when he sees* **Joan**.

Joan   *(whispering)* It's not what you think. I mean, look at him. He's an old man.

Craig   *(whispering)* So are you, Joan.

Joan   *(beat)* So I am.

Craig   *(placing cups down)* Those are yours and these are Jim's.

Joan   You know I used to believe, when I was young, that one day I would find the perfect man.

Craig   One man can never be everything you want.

Joan   Is that right? *(beat)* Did you never get caught?

Craig   Not yet.

Joan *laughs.* **Jim** *stirs.* **Joan** *freezes.* **Jim** *cuddles up to him, settles again.*

Craig   I just assumed he was straight.

Joan   Get off the apps and open your eyes up.

Craig Maybe I'll try that. Night.

Craig *leaves.* **Joan** *looks after him, then at the photo. Monteverdi's 'I Gaze at You' begins.*

Joan And when I want your opinion, I'll ask for it.

Joan *hesitates then clasps his hand around* **Jim**'s *as the music swells and lights fade.*

Scene 8

Several evenings later. The contents of Jim's case have been disbursed.

Joan It's very minimalist.

Jim Sit.

Joan (*sitting*) Don't you miss your home comforts?

Jim Home is where the heart is.

Joan Load of old rubbish.

Jim Is it?

Jim *sits.* **Joan** *spots the photograph.*

Joan Your lover?

Jim He wasn't much to look at but…

Joan You loved him?

Jim (*beat*) I did.

A knock.

Joan Who is it?

Craig (*off*) Are you decent?

Joan More or less.

Craig *comes in with two nightcaps.* **Joan** *flashes his stomach.*

Craig Ugh, gross!

Joan Because I'm not twenty-something, muscle-bound and wearing fake orange tan?

Craig Stick that in it. (*thrusting pills at Joan*) So, Jim, I see you've unpacked? (*offering pills to Jim*) Joan must be having some positive influence.

Jim He is, yes.

Jim *looks at* **Joan**. **Joan** *looks at* **Jim**. **Craig** *looks between them.*

Craig I, er… (*taking something from his pocket*) I got you a present.

Craig *throws it. Neither* **Joan** *nor* **Jim***'s reflexes are quick enough to catch the condom packet.* **Jim** *turns scarlet.*

Joan Well, I do hope they're ribbed for extra sensation.

Jim *laughs.* **Joan** *coughs.*

Jim Are you okay?

Joan *waves it off.* **Craig** *squats.*

Craig But seriously…

Joan Oh, please…

Craig I seem to have dissuaded the Taliban from having you extradited by social services…

Joan Me?

Craig (*giving Joan a look*) Principally because… Well, it appears to us that the two of you may be embarking on some sort of relationship…?

Joan *and* **Jim** *exchange a look.*

Joan Yes.

Jim Yes.

Craig So we thought we'd give you a little more time in the hope you might… settle in.

Jim Thank you.

Joan Thanks.

Craig (*standing*) Can't believe I tried to fix you up with Eileen.

Joan Eileen?

Jim Will she survive the disappointment, do you think?

Craig Let me know if you need anything. Like a prescription.

Craig *mimes an erection.* **Joan** *blushes this time.* **Craig** *laughs and exits.*

Jim I can't believe I had him down as…

Joan Straight-acting only, that one.

Jim I suppose I just assume that black men aren't…

Joan Ignorance is the mother of assumption.

Jim *(beat)* Have you…?

Joan A fair few.

Jim And do…?

Joan Not all clichés are true. *(raising his cup)* Cheers.

Jim *(raising his own)* Cheers.

They swallow their pills down. 'September' from Strauss' 'Four Last Songs' begins.

Joan Right, best get to bed then.

Jim Yours or mine?

The music swells and lights fade.

Scene 9

Autumn. Morning. **Jim** *is sleeping. The photo of his lover is now framed.* **Joan**, *in a robe, is looking out the window. His coughing wakes* **Jim**.

Jim   You're early.

Joan   Always am these days.

Jim   You okay?

Joan   I'm fine. Birds are migrating.

Jim   Is it already that time?

Jim *grunts as he tries to sit up.*

Joan   Your back?

Joan *moves to help.*

Jim   It's difficult, isn't it? The two of us in one little bed.

Joan   So you slept in the armchair instead?

A knock. They both turn to look.

Craig   (*off*) Breakfast!

Joan & **Jim**   Coming!

Joan (*kissing Jim on head*) Morning.

Jim Morning. I wonder what today will bring?

Joan (*laughing*) Well the possibilities are endless.

Joan *applies lipstick in a mirror.*

Joan We could… play cards?

Jim You're a bad loser.

Joan Watch Casablanca?

Jim Again.

Joan Perhaps we should take up knitting?

Jim We don't have any offspring.

Joan (*slapping belly*) Did I not tell you?

Jim We'll have to get married then.

Joan Only if I can wear the full meringue.

Jim Fine.

Joan (*beat*) Are you serious?

Jim I think I am.

Joan That's terribly sweet of you, young man. But I am not the marrying kind. (*blowing a kiss*) Why don't you let me do your lips?

Jim What are you afraid of?

Joan I am not afraid of anything.

Jim Except perhaps acceptance?

Joan (*beat*) I'll take that as a 'no' then.

Joan *tosses the lipstick down.*

Jim Well the offer will stand. Now let's see if I can. (*standing*) I'm glad I didn't attempt to go down on a knee or anything.

Joan How long have I been here?

Jim Is it September?

Joan And I arrived in June.

Jim About three months then.

Joan That's only how long we've known each other.

Jim It's a long time in this place.

Joan *hands* **Jim** *his stick.*

Jim Of course, we could have an open marriage.

Joan *laughs.*

Jim I know you don't do 'hetero-normative'.

Joan Girl's not got a lot of choice in this place.

Gluck's 'I've Lost My Eurydice' starts as they shuffle out.

Jim Use mine as the main room. Yours as a…

Joan Dressing room?

Jim Secret passage between the two.

Joan Or perhaps a glory hole?

Jim And then there's the double bed.

Joan Now there's an incentive.

The music swells and lights fade.

Scene 10

That evening. **Joan** *is knitting, a record spinning.*

Jim *is reading a book on ancient history. He looks up, sighs.*

Jim Just us tonight. (*to photo*) Have you minded very much, sitting there watching us? (*laughing*) You've probably enjoyed it, kinky bastard. (*beat*) Remember the time you wanted to bring that boy back and I wasn't having any of it? (*beat*) That sort of thing wasn't for me. Still isn't, really. (*beat*) I suspect you had him anyway.

A knock.

Jim Come in.

Craig *comes in with two nightcaps.*

Craig Where's Joan?

Jim In his room.

Craig You two had a row or something?

Jim Joan just needed some Joan time.

Craig *offers* **Jim** *a cup.* **Jim** *takes the pills.* **Craig** *contemplates the photo on the cabinet.*

Craig How long were you guys together?

Jim It would have been thirty years…

Craig Thirty!

Jim He died a few months before.

Craig That's such a long time.

Jim How long have you been…?

Craig Three in December, if we make it that far.

Jim Lot of give-and-take, to stay together.

Jim *hands the cup back.*

Craig Yeah.

Craig *heads out.*

Jim You know, if there's something you want to tell me about…?

Craig Night!

Jim Night.

Craig Hey, at least you'll get some sleep.

Craig *exits.*

Jim I doubt it.

Joan I'd forgotten that. Was it…

Jim (*to photo*) You know, I never got used to the emptiness on your side of the mattress.

Joan (*to photo*) Seventy-one, I think. Around the time of The Festival of Light. Fucking bitch.

Jim I would reach out in my sleep and wake empty-handed. And in that second between sleeping and waking, lose you all over again.

Joan We staged that mock-wedding protest. Jeremy and I fought over who should wear the dress. (*laughing*) I wonder what happened to it?

Jim Here goes nothing.

Jim *turns the light out.*

A knock.

Joan Who is it?

Craig (*off*) Room service.

Craig *comes in.*

Joan Thought I'd have you to myself tonight. What do you think?

Craig What is it?

Joan Lemon twin set. Age appropriate.

Craig *doesn't laugh, offers pill cup.*

Joan Nice pearl necklace to go with it.

Still **Craig** *doesn't laugh.*

Joan What's up with you tonight?

Joan *knocks the pills back.*

Craig I got caught.

Joan Ah.

Craig Yeah.

Joan (*beat*) In flagrante delicto?

Craig (*beat*) He looked at my phone.

Joan (*handing cup back*) So…?

Craig Don't know. See when I get home.

Craig *heads out.*

Joan Did he tell you he proposed to me?

Craig Really?

Craig *stops.* **Joan** *nods.*

Craig You didn't accept?

Joan Of course not.

Craig Did you even consider it?

Joan Darling, marriage is an antiquated patriarchal institution designed for the control of women: why on earth would I give it my consideration?

Craig Or perhaps Joan, marriage—at this time, in this place—is the most radical action you could possibly take?

Joan (*beat*) You think?

Craig I think I'm going to ask him to be open.

Joan And how do you think that'll go down?

Craig I hope he will at least give it his consideration. Sweet dreams.

Craig *leaves. The waltz from 'Swan Lake' begins.*

Joan Of course, it might be worth it just to see The Taliban's face. (*laughing*) Perhaps she could be bridesmaid…

The music swells and lights fade.

Scene 11

Night. A few weeks later. The rooms have joined together. **Jim**, *in dapper tie, offers his hand to* **Joan**, *in delicious frock.* **Joan** *takes it. They're wearing matching costume rings.*

Jim Will you be the woman?

Joan Can't I just be Joan?

They dance, magically, as if half their ages.

Joan Does this mean I'm finally a swan?

Jim You were never an ugly duckling.

As the music calms, their frailties return and they lay back on a double-bed.

Joan I thought it went rather well in the end.

Jim A good time had by all and everyone. Even Eileen.

Joan I think that may have had something to do with the fizzy wine.

Jim I did see the Taliban redistributing several glasses in her direction.

Joan And of course, the bouquet.

Jim Did you hit her deliberately?

Joan You may be overestimating my wrist action.

Jim Nothing wrong with it in my experience.

Joan *starts laughing, coughing.*

Joan It's nothing. Too much rich food and dancing.

Jim You barely ate anything.

Joan I was saving some room.

Joan *pulls* **Jim** *by the tie.*

Jim Mm...

They kiss.

Joan Lovely mattress.

Jim Orthopaedic.

Joan We pay extra for that?

Jim A civil service pension has its advantages.

A knock. They readjust themselves.

Jim Come in!

Craig *(off)* Is this the bridal suite?

Craig *comes in, wearing something celebratory. He has a tray in one hand and the other behind his back.*

Jim I'm afraid we haven't broken the hymen yet.

Craig I have something that might help with that. (*putting down the nightcaps*) One extra tonight.

Joan You got it?

Jim What's that?

Joan You'll find out soon.

Craig It's the blue one. I got you something else too…

Craig *pulls a cake from behind his back. Two grooms sit lopsided atop it.*

Craig In fact, I made it for you.

Jim Look at that!

Joan Is that a (*mouthing*) hash cake?

Craig Only the finest ingredients.

Craig *puts it on the cabinet.*

Joan Delicious.

Jim Thank you. (*taking Craig's hand*) Thanks for everything.

Craig Where did you get that ring?

Jim Ebay. Bargain.

Craig My tutoring paid off then. Have fun!

Craig *leaves. 'At Sunset', the last of Strauss' 'Four Last Songs' begins.* **Joan** *rubs his chest again.*

Jim How you feeling?

Joan I'm fine.

Jim This corset won't be helping.

Jim *struggles to unlace it.*

Joan Such a lovely man. Where have you been all my lifetime?

Jim I'm here now, Joan. How do you undo this thing?

The music swells and lights focus. **Joan** *walks into the light, looks at* **Jim**, *then into the light again, spreads his wings, and flies.*

Scene 12

Several months later. Morning. **Jim**, *still suited, is stood by the record player, listening, looking between the pictures of Alex and Joan.*

Jim   Look out for each other.

Jim, *slowly, with difficulty knots his black tie, checks it in the mirror and sees Joan's lipstick, hesitates, reaches for it, removes the lid, winds it, raises it towards his lips.*

A knock. **Jim** *lowers the lipstick.*

Jim   Come in.

The door opens. **Craig** *is there, wearing black.*

Craig   Bus is ready. The others are all loaded.

Jim   Do you know how to do this?

Craig *hesitates, nods, takes the lipstick, applies it.*

Craig   There.

Jim *rubs his lips together, looks in the mirror.* **Craig** *hesitates, applies the stick to his own lips.* **Jim** *turns to see him.*

Jim   Well look at you.

Craig *smiles, puts lipstick down.*

Craig We should go.

Craig *offers his arm.* **Jim** *takes it.*

Jim Thank you.

They exit. The music swells and lights fade.

Acknowledgements

Thank you to Justin David, Polly Wiseman,
Jacqueline Haigh, Simon Brown and Pippa Brill
for their support in the writing.

Thank you to Andrew Ellerby, Catia Ciarico,
David Sheppeard, Alexis Gregory, John Atterbury,
The King's Head Theatre, The Nursery, Clive Lyttle,
Bryan McIntosh-Melville, Gary Davy, Richard Meredith
and Raiomond Mirza for their support in the production.

Thank you to Jason Dowler, Zorian Clayton, Alice Holland,
Angela Ellis, Glenda Evans, John Evans, David Duchin,
Walter Cabell, Gabriel Vogt, Lloyd Vanata, David Upton,
Amanda Lyon, Daren Kay, Nic Alderton, Beverley Angel,
David Walters, Bevis Jones, Anna Sutton, Tessa Garland,
Kit de Waal, Liz Norton, Max Barber, Piers Torday
for their support in the fundraising.

Thank you to Ben Walters, Opening Doors London and
Mosaic LGBT Youth Centre for their participation
in the post-show discussion.

Thank you to Holly Revell and Alice Evans
for filming and photographing. Thank you to our
technical and front of house teams.

And thank you to Genet for his *Song of Love*.

Also from Inkandescent

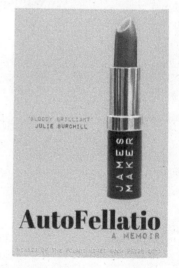

Progressive books for enlightened readers

Inkandescent Publishing was created in 2016 by Justin David and Nathan Evans to shine a light on diverse and distinctive voices. Sign up to our mailing list to stay informed about future releases:

www.inkandescent.co.uk

Follow us on Facebook:

@InkandescentPublishing

and on Twitter:

@InkandescentUK